Magic Words

Story and Illustrations
by Frances McAliley

Published in the United States of America
Brilliant Books Literary
137 Forest Park Lane Thomasville
North Carolina 27360 USA

ISBN:
Paperback: 979-8-88945-290-4
Ebook: 979-8-88945-291-1
Hardback: 979-8-88945-292-8

# THE MAGIC WORDS

by FRANCES J. McALILEY

In the home of Susan and Jim Doright, life was always impossible.

They had two unbearable children – Billy and Mary.
These children screamed, stomped and demanded
something from morning to night.

Susan couldn't wait until the children were in bed.  That
was the only time the house was quiet.

Jim couldn't wait until he left for work. That was
when he had peace.

Jim and Susan never went out alone because they couldn't get babysitters.

They didn't go out as a family because the children
caused so much commotion that they were asked to leave
restaurants and movies.

At amusement parks everyone stared at them. They would be so embarassed, they would leave on their own.

Something had to be done!

One night Susan and Jim sat down after the little terrors were in bed. Susan said, "I can't take it any more!"

Jim said, "Let's run away!"

Susan replied, "We can't do that. No one would take care of Mary and Billy.

We must teach our children to be mannerly, patient, and kind."

Jim said, "How are we going to do that?"

Susan thought for a moment before she answered. "Let's play a game with them. A magic game. We will call it the 'Magic Word Game.' When something happens or they want something, they must use the magic words. If they don't use the magic words, they will become invisible. We will not be able to see or hear them."

Interested, Jim asked, "It sounds like a good idea, but do you think it will work?"

"We don't have a choice. We have to try something!" she replied.

So Susan and Jim worked out the rules for the game, and decided to begin to play the next day.

The next morning when the children came down to breakfast, Billy shouted, "Daddy, tie my shoes! Tie my shoes now!"

Mary shouted, " I want my hair combed now!"

Calmly mother said, "Children, sit down. We want to talk to you. We are not happy with the way you behave. We want you to be kind to us, to each other, and to others. We want you to speak softly and politely.

We want you to be patient and wait for us to do things for you. Most of all, we want you to say the magic words – please, thank you, excuse me, and I'm sorry.

"To make this fun, we are going to play a game. We will call the game, 'Magic Words.' When you are screaming, fighting, rude or throwing a tantrum, you will become invisible, and Father and I will not be able to see or hear you.

"When you improve your behavior, and use the magic words, you will get hugs and kisses."

Billy and Mary shouted at the same time, "We don't want to play your dumb, old game!"

Mother just got up and walked toward the kitchen.

At the door of the kitchen, she turned and said,

"When you are bad,
You make me sad.
You will become invisible and disappear
So the bad things I can't see or hear.
The good things you do,
and the magic words you say
Will make the spell go away!"

In the kitchen mother started to cook breakfast. Mary and Billy followed her. They sat at the table and began repeatedly to shout their demands as usual.

"I want cereal!" shouted Billy.

"I want pancakes!" shouted Mary.

Without turning, mother repeated her magic word rhyme.

When you are bad,
You make me sad.
You will become invisible and disappear
So the bad things I can't see or hear.
The good things you do,
and the magic words you say
Will make the spell go away!

Mother put the bread in the toaster and poured the juice. She cooked the eggs and bacon. She set the table. During all of this, Mary and Billy continued to shout and bang on the table.

Mother said nothing. She put breakfast on the table for Father and herself. They began to eat.

Billy and Mary were shocked. They stopped banging and shouting and stared at their parents eating without them.

This had never happened before.

They were used to Mother screaming at them, and Father giving them what they wanted. Watching their parents eat was making them hungrier. They both ran out of the kitchen crying. This always got what they wanted.

In the living room, they waited, but nothing happened. They could hear Mother and Father talking softly about what they had planned for the day.

After breakfast the children were playing in their room, when Mother heard screaming. She ran up the steps to see what was wrong as usual, but did not scream as usual.

Instead, as she watched the children pushing,
pulling and shouting, she said,

When you are bad,
You make me sad.
You will become invisible and disappear
So the bad things, I can't see or hear.
The good things you do,
and the magic words you say
Will make the spell go away!

Mother left the room, but she stood outside the door where she couldn't be seen. She heard the children stop crying and shouting. They looked at each other. Something was wrong! Mother was acting different. She was too calm. Then they remembered what she had said before she left the room. She had made them invisible.

Billy looked at Mary and said, "I'm sorry, Mary. Suppose we share the truck. We can play together."

"That's a good idea!" replied Mary, "I'm sorry, too."

Mother was so happy to see her children playing together that she rushed into the room and gave each child a hug.

That night after Susan and Jim had tucked the children into bed, they sat and talked about the day. Things were getting better around the house. The tantrums had just about stopped. The "Magic Word Game" was working!

Susan and Jim decided to reward the children by taking them out to dinner the next day.

When Jim came home from work, Susan, Billy, and Mary were ready and eager to go.

At the car, Mary started shouting, "I want to sit on that side of the car behind Mother!" Before Billy could answer, Mother said,

When you are bad,

You make me sad.

You will become invisible and disappear

So the bad things I can't see or hear.

The good things you do,

and the magic words you say

Will make the spell go away!

Automatically Billy said, "All right, Mary, I will sit on this side."

Mary said, "Thank you, Billy."

Father gave both children a hug and kiss before they entered the car.

The children talked softly to each other in the back seat instead of their usual screaming and fighting. Susan and Jim were enjoying the drive to the restaurant.

Inside the restaurant, Billy pushed Mary and said, "I'm sitting next to Mother!"

Before Mary could start crying and objecting to Billy's demand, Mother said,

When you are bad,

You make me sad.

You will become invisible and disappear

So the bad things I can't see or hear.

The good things you do,

and the magic words you say

Will make the spell go away!

Instead of crying and causing a commotion, Mary said, "O.K., Billy, I'll sit with Father."

Billy was embarrassed for pushing, and said, "I'm sorry for pushing you, Mary."

Susan and Jim hugged the children and looked at each other and smiled before they sat down.

The Dorights enjoyed their dinner without tantrums. The children were behaving better. Even the waitress told the children how well they behaved.

Susan and Jim promised the children they would take them to the amusement park on the weekend if they continued their good behavior.

Billy said, " Mother, I like the Magic Word Game!"

"Yeah," added Mary, "We get to go out to restaurants and amusement parks."

Mother said, " I like the Magic Word Game also. I don't have to scream, shout, and get upset everyday."

Father said, "I enjoy being with my family more since the game."

There were no problems on the drive home.

All week, the whole family was looking forward to the weekend trip.

When Saturday finally arrived, the children were very good. They got up, dressed, and were no problem at breakfast.

After mother finished the breakfast dishes, the family got into the car to drive to the amusement park.

As the Dorights entered the park, Mother said,

When you are bad,

You make me sad.

You will become invisible and disappear

So the bad things I can't see or hear.

The good things you do,

and the magic words you say

Will make the spell go away!


Billy said, "What have we done?"


Mary said, "We have been good all week!"


Mother hugged them both and said, "I thought
I'd just remind you."

Mary and Billy were so good, that people who passed the Dorights said, "What nice children."

The whole family had a great time riding and eating.

As the Dorights left the park, Billy hugged and kissed his parents, and said, "Thank you, Mother and Father, for taking us to the park."

Mary said, as she hugged her parents, "You are the best parents in the world!"

"Now that you are polite and use the Magic Words," Mother replied, "You are the best children in the world. You have learned that

What you say
Helps you get your way!"